400 Floral Motifs for Designers, Needleworkers and Craftspeople

From the Wm. Briggs and Company Ltd. "Album of Transfer Patterns"

Edited by Carol Belanger Grafton

Dover Publications, Inc.
New York

Copyright © 1986 by Dover Publications, Inc.
All rights reserved under Pan American and International Copyright Conventions.

Published in Canada by General Publishing Company, Ltd., 30 Lesmill Road, Don Mills, Toronto, Ontario.
Published in the United Kingdom by Constable and Company, Ltd.

This Dover edition, first published in 1986, is a selection from the Wm. Briggs and Company Ltd. *Album of Transfer Patterns* [n.d., circa 1900?]. This Dover edition contains an introduction with instructions for transferring designs and a description of embroidery stitches.

DOVER *Pictorial Archive* SERIES

Manufactured in the United States of America
Dover Publications, Inc., 31 East 2nd Street, Mineola, N.Y. 11501

Library of Congress Cataloging-in-Publication Data

400 floral motifs for designers, needleworkers, and craftspeople.

(Dover pictorial archive series)
1. Embroidery—Patterns. 2. Decoration and ornament. 3. House furnishings. I. Grafton, Carol Belanger. II. Wm. Briggs and Company. Album of transfer patterns. Selections. III. Title: Four hundred floral motifs for designers, needle-workers, and craftspeople. IV. Series.
TT771.A14   1986   746.44′   86-6374
ISBN 0-486-25162-4

INTRODUCTION

Although this collection of fine turn-of-the-century designs has been edited and published especially for the needleworker who is looking for something more artistically valid than what is customarily available, it is full of designs that will appeal to a host of other craftspeople as well. Originally intended to be embroidered on table mats, dresser scarfs and "D'Oylies," these designs are eminently suitable as decorations on pillows, eyeglass cases, handbags, blue jeans and dozens of other objects in constant use today. However, many of the designs are so attractive and carefully worked out that they are very successful simply as pictures to be framed and hung.

As rich and varied as this archive is, happily you are not limited to choosing and executing a single design. In fact, one of the best features of the collection is that the designs complement each other beautifully, and thereby invite you to invent your own composition by combining elements from different plates. Adding your personal color scheme and appropriate stitches from your repertory, you will have the satisfaction of creating a truly original design. After you have created several compositions from this material, you may find yourself in the enviable position of being able to design completely on your own.

The Table of Contents of this volume is organized according to motif and *suggested* uses. We emphasize "suggested" because we hope you will feel free to use your own imagination in order to get the designs to work for you.

As this is primarily a sourcebook of designs and design ideas, we do not attempt to cover the fascinating intricacies of the craft itself, which are now well described in numerous publications. However, we do want to explain how to transfer designs to fabric as well as to illustrate several basic stitches and offer a few suggestions on how to make the best use of them.

After you have chosen the design and decided upon its purpose, select and prepare the background fabric. Choose a fabric that is compatible with the design and suitable for the intended use. Pictures that are to be framed and hung on a wall may never have to be washed or take hard wear, and so can be done on delicate fabrics; but drapes or pillows will get soiled and thus require sturdier material. If you are not sure of the washability of a fabric, test a small piece before you spend valuable time embroidering it. Remember that a test by gentle hand-washing in cold water with special soap does not necessarily mean that the finished piece can be tossed into the washer! After determining suitability and/or washability, make sure the fabric is clean and pressed. Avoid using materials from which you are unable to remove creases; a crease which does not iron out before the embroidering will remain.

Next, cut the fabric to size, being careful to allow for seams, hems or the fold-over necessary if you plan to mount the piece. Make sure the cuts are "on the straight" of the fabric by pulling out a guide thread in each direction and then cutting along these lines; do not depend upon a ruler line since the fabric may have been pulled out of shape. If a piece is still out of square after cutting, take the time to dampen and press it over again. If the fabric ravels badly, it is wise to whip the edges by hand with an overcast stitch or run a large zigzag machine stitch along the edges.

Once you have chosen a design and fabric for a project, follow these simple steps to bring your work to a successful conclusion:

Step 1. Gather the materials needed for transferring and embroidering.
  You will need:

  Tracing paper
  Large piece of cardboard (oak tag or tablet back)
  Straight pins
  Tracing wheel, dull pencil or other stylus
  Ruler
  Dressmaker's carbon paper (in a color that contrasts with the color of the fabric)
  Flat smooth surface (such as a table)
  Background fabric
  Threads (yarns) for embroidery
  Embroidery tools (frame, needles, thimble, scissors, etc.)

Step 2. Make a tracing by putting a sheet of tracing paper over the design and drawing over each line with a lead pencil. We do not advise tracing directly from the book onto the fabric because the page might tear and render the designs on the overleaf page unusable.

Step 3. Transfer the design. Place the cardboard on a flat surface; this not only protects the surface of the table from scarring under the pressure of the tracing wheel, but also provides the firm padding under the fabric necessary to produce a smooth line. Carefully position your tracing on the fabric and pin it at the four corners. If the design is to be centered, use a ruler to determine the midpoint.

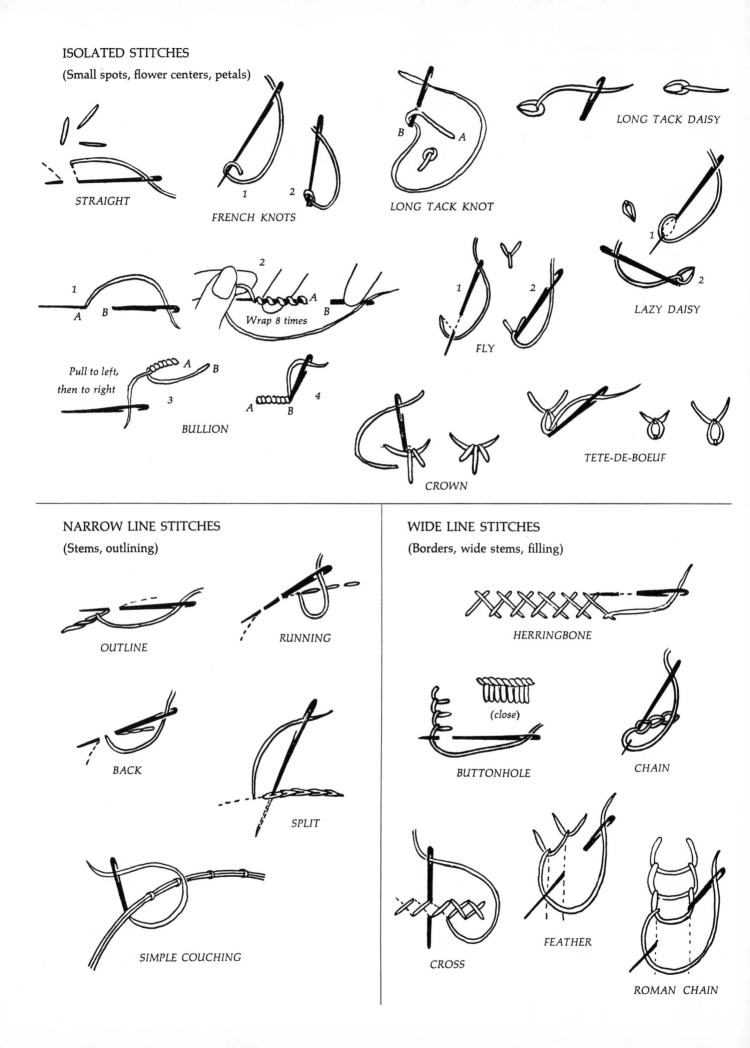

ISOLATED STITCHES
(Small spots, flower centers, petals)

STRAIGHT

FRENCH KNOTS
1   2

LONG TACK KNOT
B   A

LONG TACK DAISY

1   B
A   B
Wrap 8 times
A   B

FLY
1   2

LAZY DAISY
1
2

Pull to left, then to right
3
BULLION
A   B
A   B   4

CROWN

TETE-DE-BOEUF

NARROW LINE STITCHES
(Stems, outlining)

OUTLINE

RUNNING

BACK

SPLIT

SIMPLE COUCHING

WIDE LINE STITCHES
(Borders, wide stems, filling)

HERRINGBONE

(close)

BUTTONHOLE

CHAIN

CROSS

FEATHER

ROMAN CHAIN

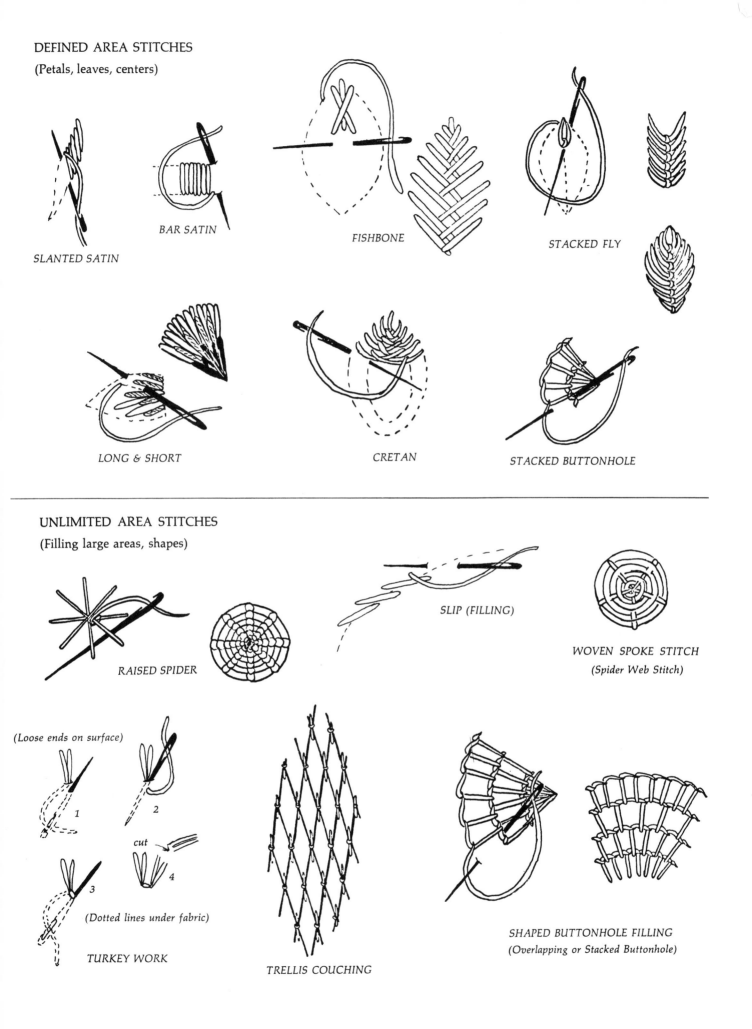

DEFINED AREA STITCHES
(Petals, leaves, centers)

SLANTED SATIN

BAR SATIN

FISHBONE

STACKED FLY

LONG & SHORT

CRETAN

STACKED BUTTONHOLE

UNLIMITED AREA STITCHES
(Filling large areas, shapes)

RAISED SPIDER

SLIP (FILLING)

WOVEN SPOKE STITCH
(Spider Web Stitch)

(Loose ends on surface)

1

2

cut

3

4

(Dotted lines under fabric)

TURKEY WORK

TRELLIS COUCHING

SHAPED BUTTONHOLE FILLING
(Overlapping or Stacked Buttonhole)

Slip the carbon, color-side down, between the tracing and the fabric, temporarily removing one of the corner pins if necessary. Do *not* use typewriter carbon; it will smudge and rub off on the fabric and is almost impossible to remove. Dressmaker's carbon, available at notions, fabric and dime stores, comes in packs of assorted colors in strips about 7 × 20 inches. It has a hard waxy finish and is designed for our purpose. Do not pin the carbon in place. With a hard, even pressure, trace a few lines with a tracing wheel or similar tool. Raise one corner of the tracing and the carbon to check the impression. If the results are too faint, apply more pressure; if too heavy, less pressure. Too heavy a line is difficult to hide with embroidery and too light a line is hard to see, but keep in mind that the transfer does have a tendency to fade a bit as it is handled and so should be a little on the heavy side. After adjusting the impression, trace the entire design and then remove the carbon and all but two pins. Carefully lift one side of the tracing paper and check to make sure the design is intact on the fabric *before removing the pattern*. Once removed, it is almost impossible to register the pattern to the fabric again.

If later on, during the embroidery process, the line becomes too faint, touch it up with a waterproof felt-tip pen or a laundry marker. Test the pen! If it is not waterproof it will run and ruin your embroidery; just the moisture from a steam iron is enough to cause this. (A pencil can be used unless you are working with light-colored yarns which the lead could discolor.)

That's all there is to the basic method of transferring designs. You are now ready to embroider. Keep in mind that the success of your embroidery depends, like a good marriage, on the compatibility of its component parts—a happy wedding of design, fabric, thread and stitches.

CONTENTS
and Index of Uses

(The individual motifs have been identified on the plates wherever possible.)

Type of Design	Suggested Uses	Page
Borders		1
Narrow	Eyeglass case covers, tablecloths, bed linens, guest towels, clothing	
Medium and Wide	Wall hangings, tablecloths, drapes, clothing	
Corners, Centers and Powderings		33
Small	Pillows, tablecloths, bed linens, guest towels, handbags	
Large	Pillows, tablecloths, drapes	
Allover Patterns	Pillows, quilt squares, drapes	56
Wreaths	Frames, bed linens, guest towels, pincushions	61
Birds and Butterflies	Accents, combinations	71
Tablecloth Centers and Cushion Squares	Pillows, cushions, tablecloths, quilt squares	83
Sprays	Pillows, tablecloths, bed linens, guest towels, clothing	102
Index of Motifs		119

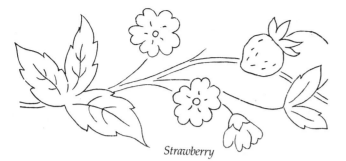

Strawberry

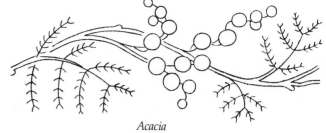

Acacia

Primrose and Hawthorn

Wild Rose and Jessamine

Ivy and Daisy

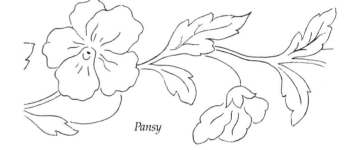

Pansy

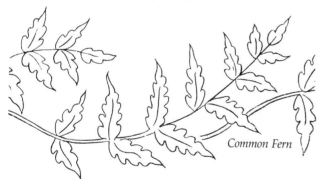

Common Fern

Apple Blossom

Daisy and Mountain Ash

Azalea

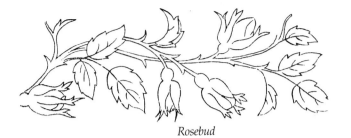

Rosebud

Jessamine

Mountain Ash

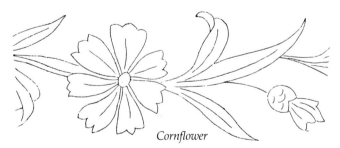

Ivy

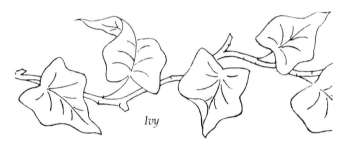

Fern

Wild Rose

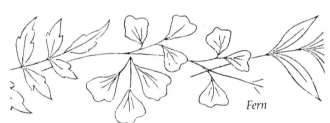

Cornflower

Daisy

Forget-Me-Not and Fern

Forget-Me-Not and Rosebud

Forget-Me-Not

Mountain Ash

Rosebud and Leaf

Hawthorn Blossom

Ox-Eye Daisy

Passion Flower

Lilium

Mountain Ash

Acorn

Fuchsia

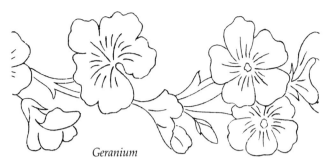

Geranium

Jessamine

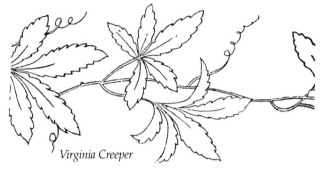

Virginia Creeper

Holly with Berries

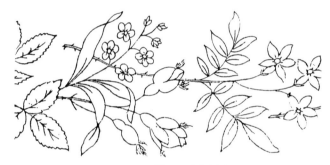

Rose, Jessamine and Forget-Me-Not

Cherry

Daisy and Fern

Marguerite Daisy

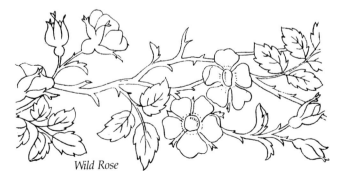

Wild Rose

Sycamore

Virginia Creeper

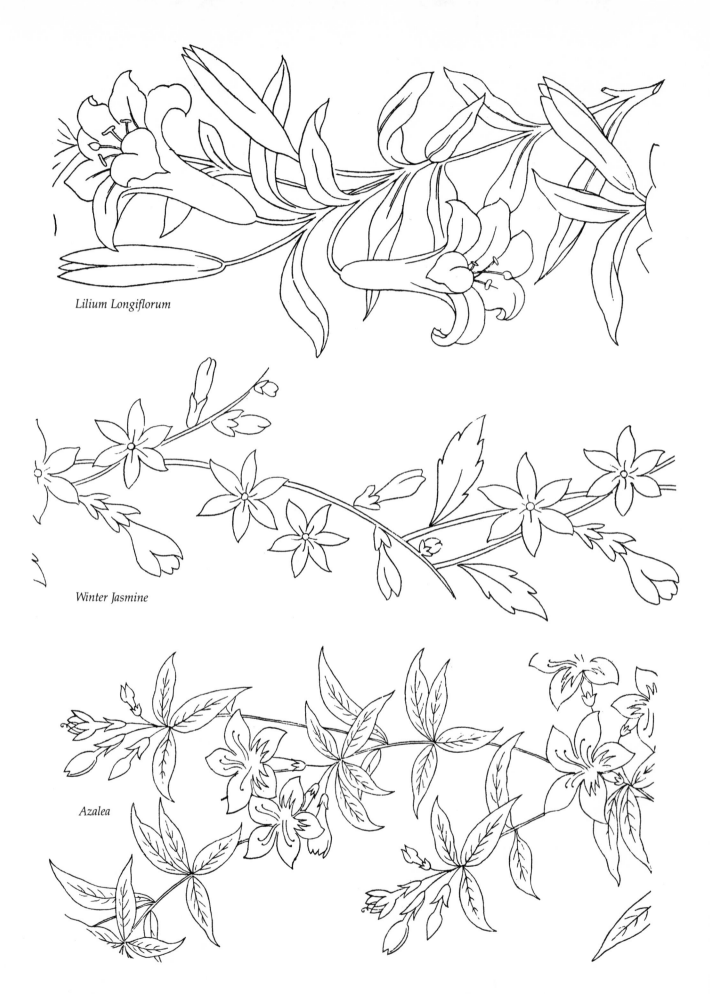

Lilium Longiflorum

Winter Jasmine

Azalea

Renaissance

Orange

Narcissus and Forget-Me-Not

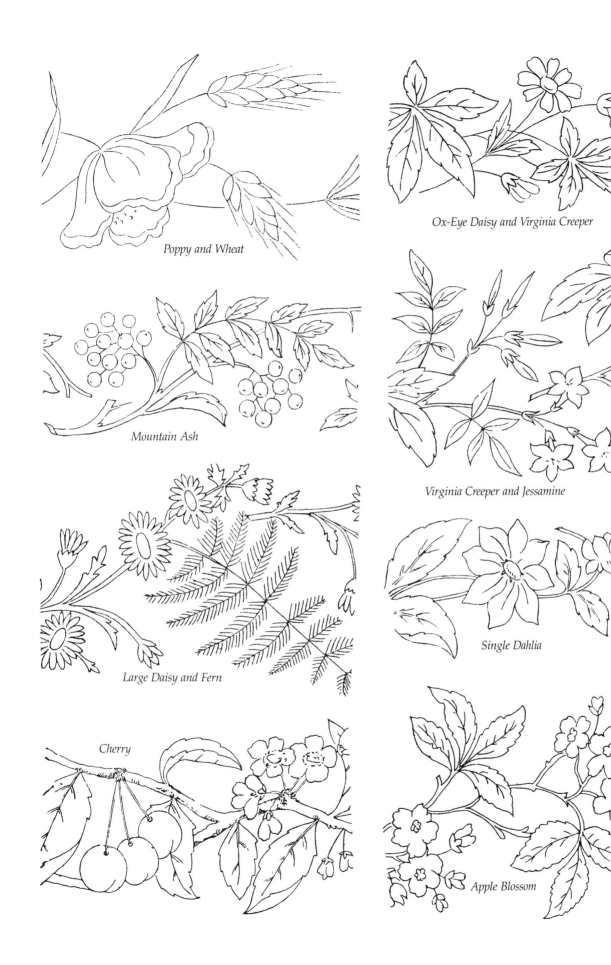

Poppy and Wheat

Ox-Eye Daisy and Virginia Creeper

Mountain Ash

Virginia Creeper and Jessamine

Large Daisy and Fern

Single Dahlia

Cherry

Apple Blossom

Lozenge

Ox-Eye Daisy and Carnation

Poppy

Forget-Me-Not

Poppy

Mixed Leaves

Ox-Eye Daisy

Fuchsia

Wild Rose

Lilium

Fuchsia and Fern

Conventional Marguerite Daisy

Wild Rose and Maidenhair

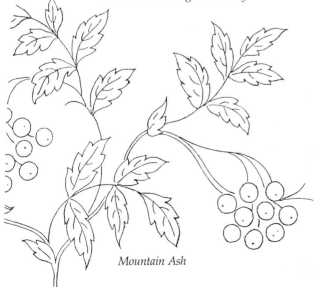

Mountain Ash

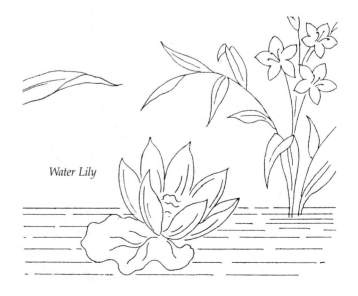

Water Lily

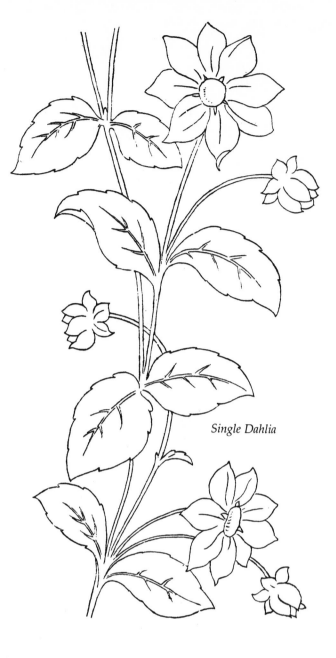

Single Dahlia

Pomegranate

Hibiscus

Daffodil and Crocus

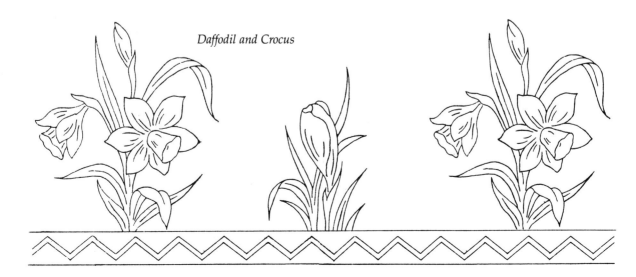

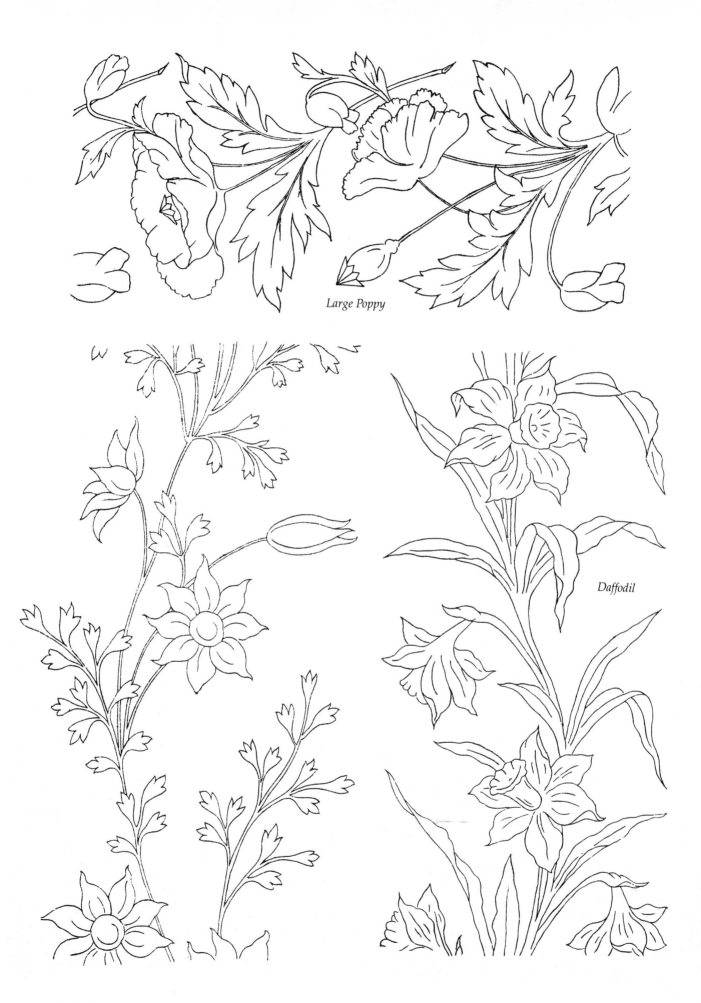

Large Poppy

Daffodil

Marguerite Daisy

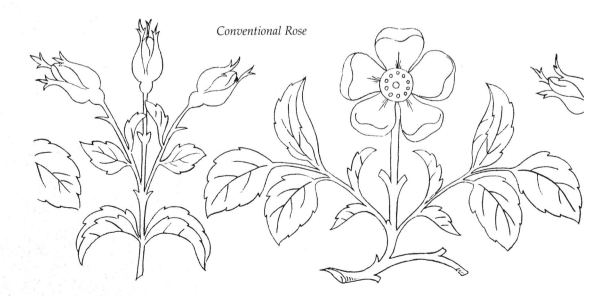

Conventional Rose

Poppy

Water Lily

Pansy Festoon

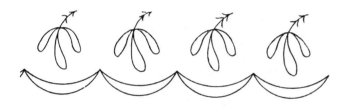

Blush Rose

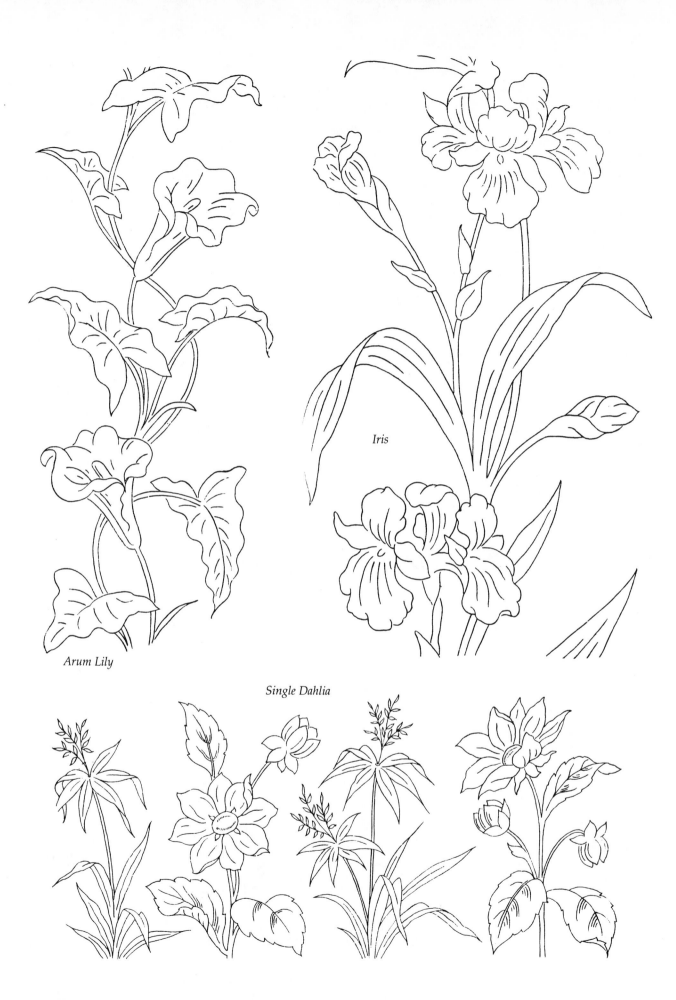

Iris

Arum Lily

Single Dahlia

Iris

Poppy

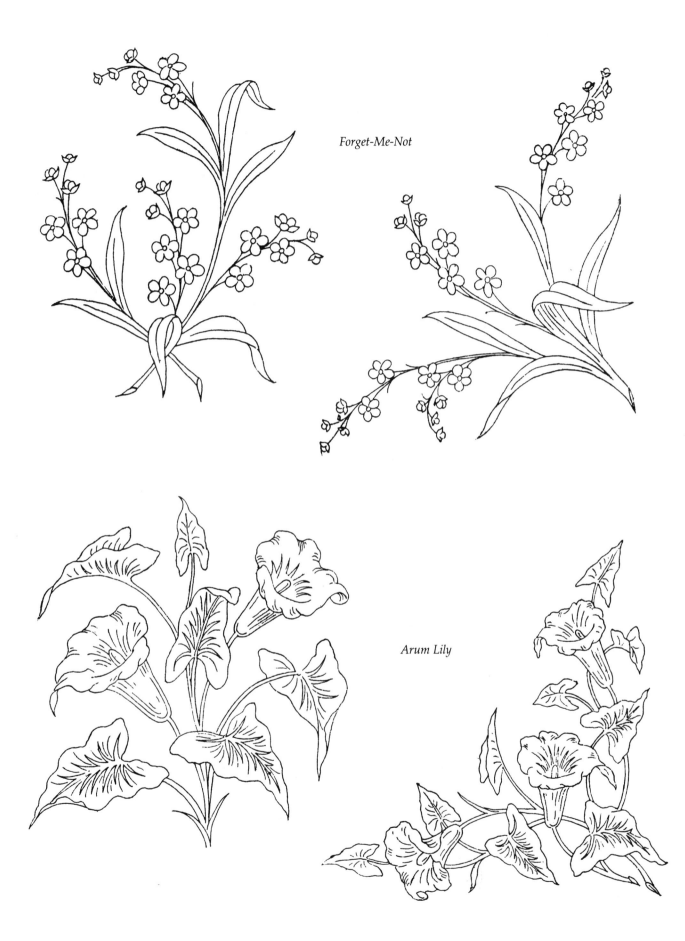

Forget-Me-Not

Arum Lily

Passion Flower

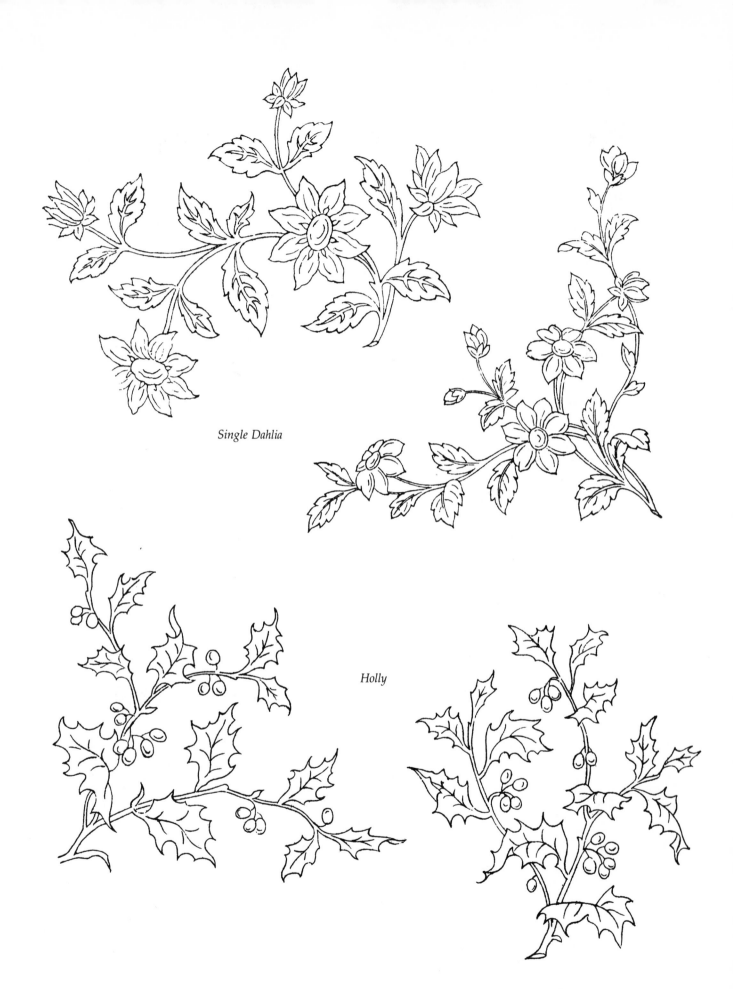

Single Dahlia

Holly

Wild Rose

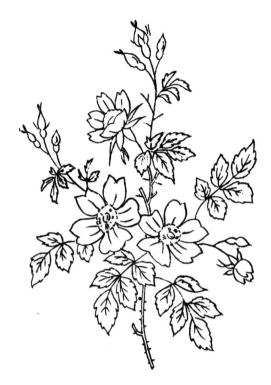

Maidenhair and Fern

Lily

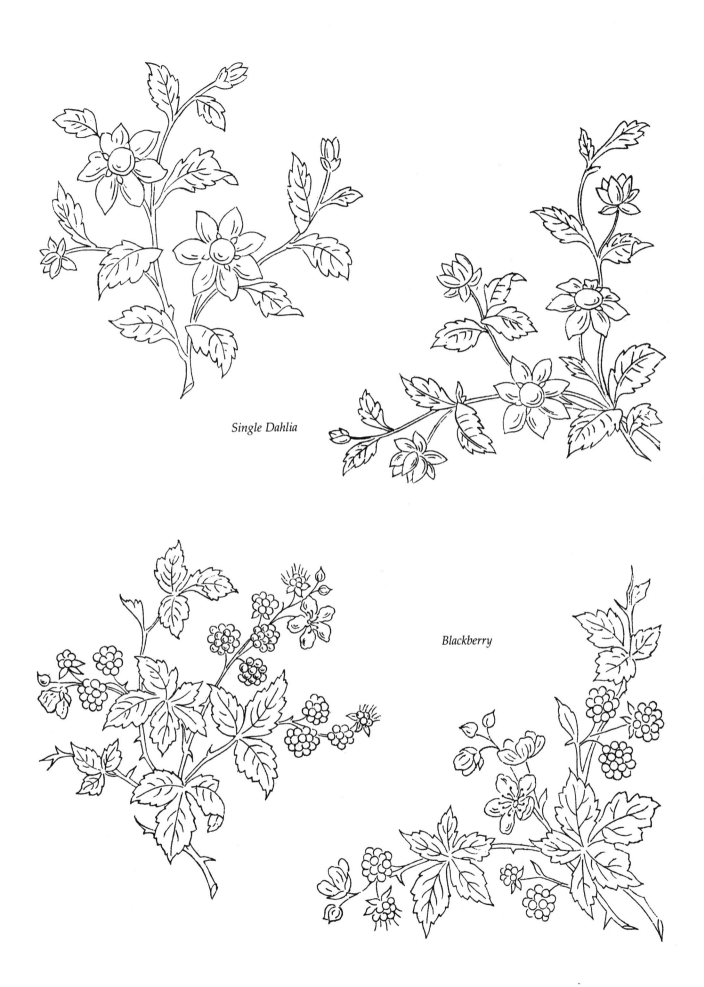

Single Dahlia

Blackberry

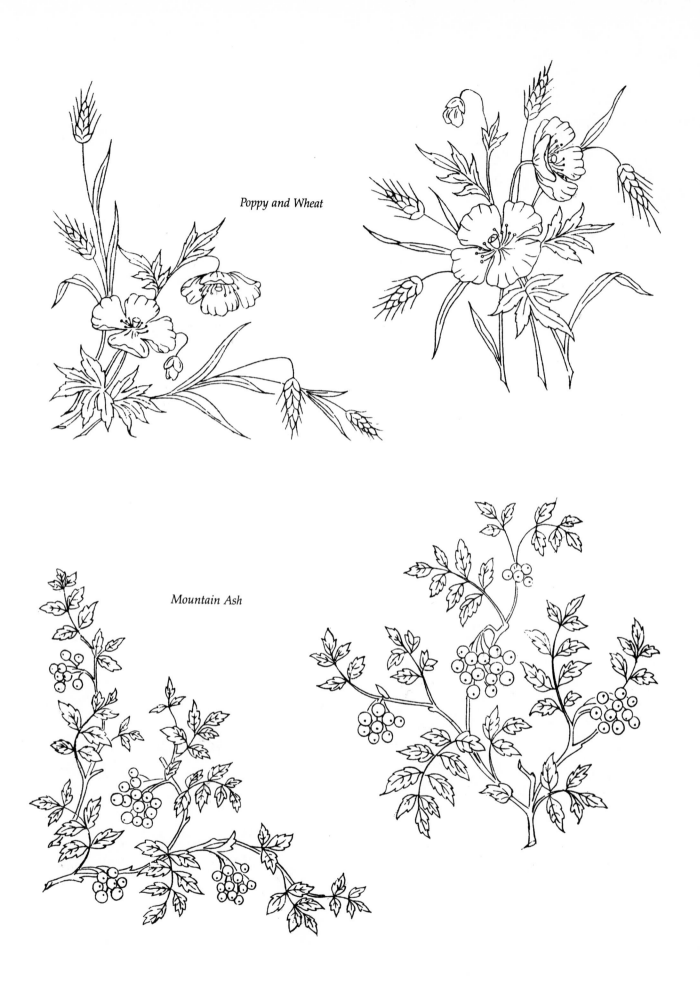

Poppy and Wheat

Mountain Ash

Apple Blossom

Fuchsia

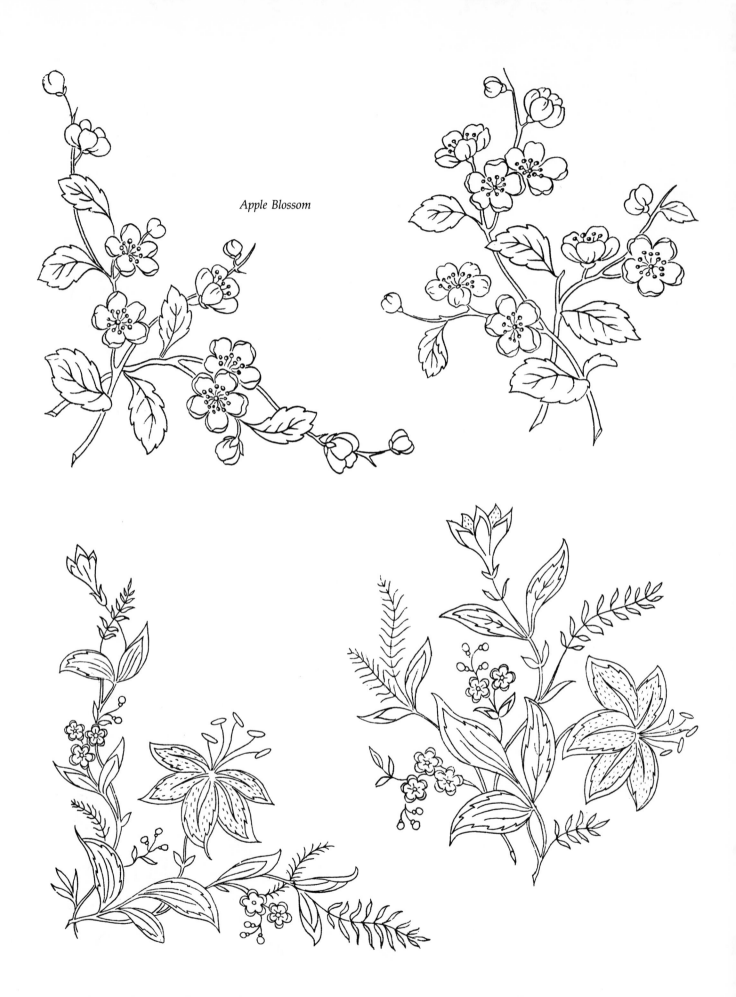

Apple Blossom

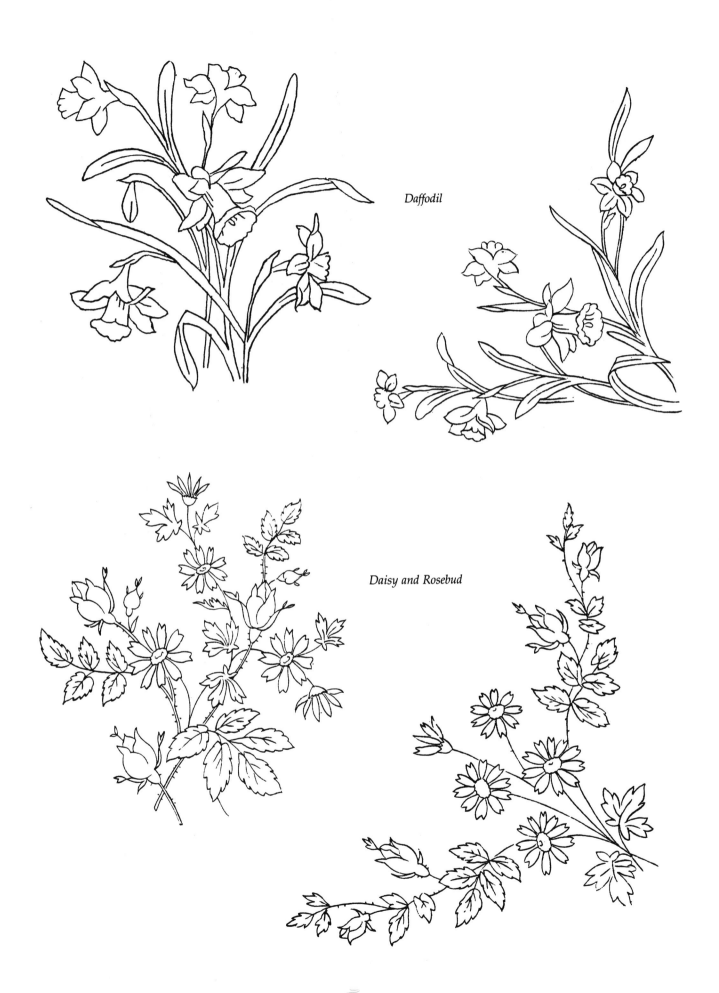

Daffodil

Daisy and Rosebud

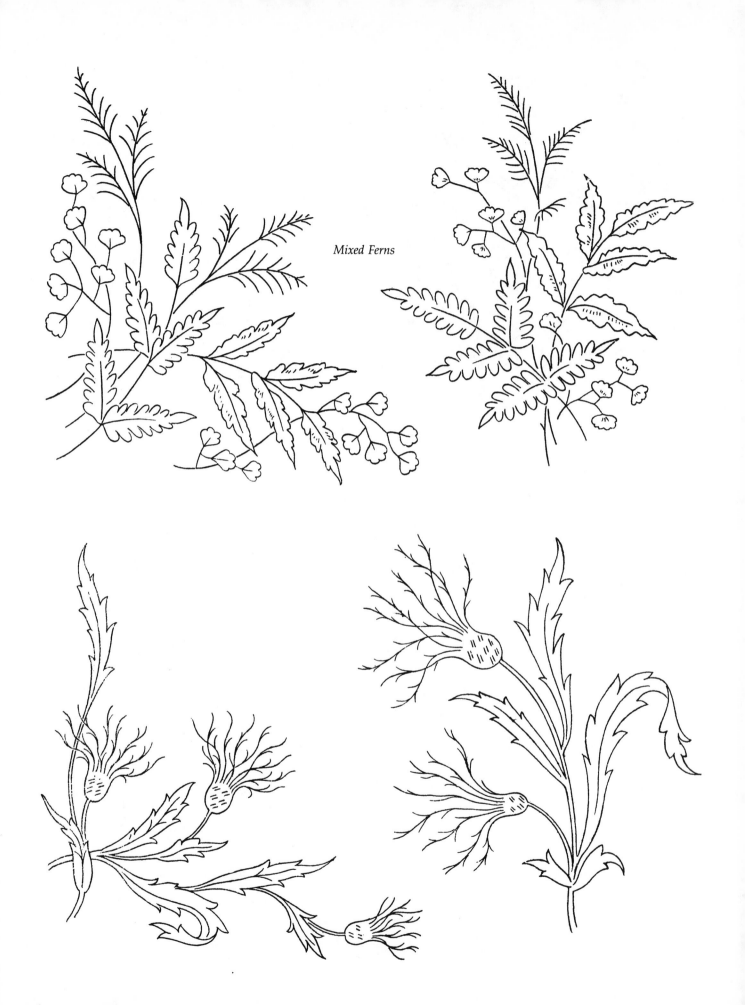

Mixed Ferns

Clover

Cyclamen

Single Dahlia

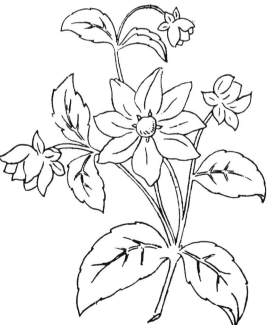

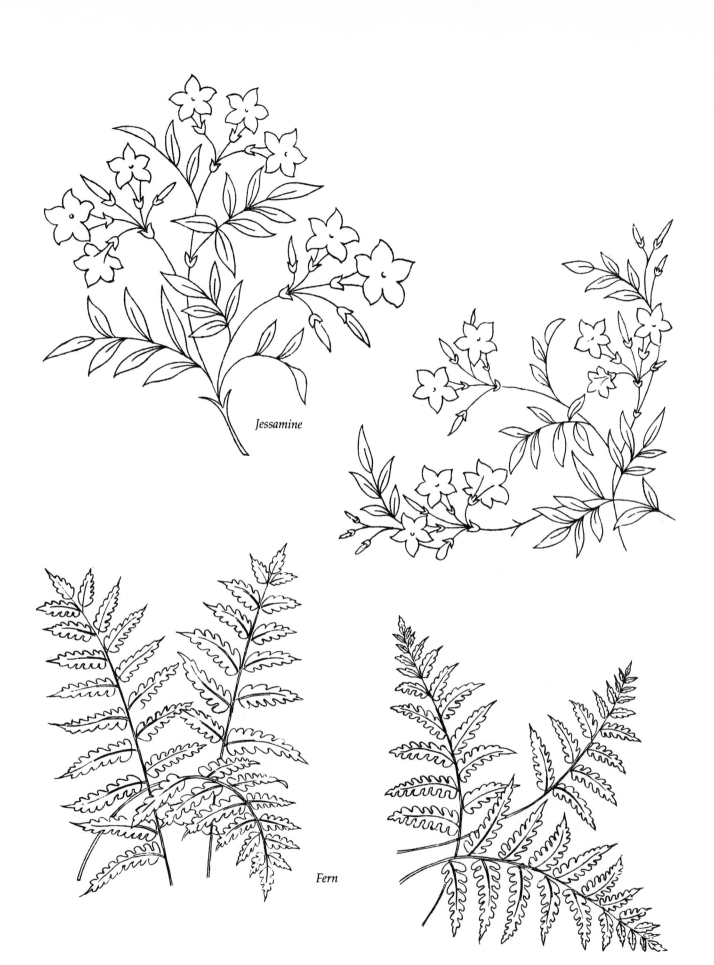

Jessamine

Fern

Daffodil

Rosebud and Forget-Me-Not

Virginia Creeper

Mountain Ash

Rosebud and Daisy

Blackberry

Begonia

Hawthorn

Strawberry

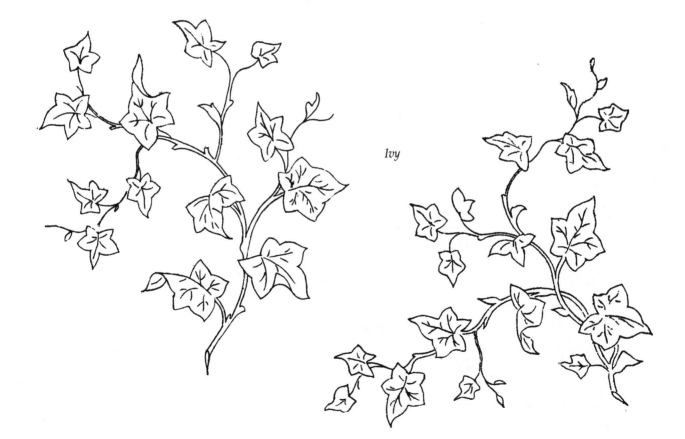

Ivy

Pink

Pansy and Daisy

Single Dahlia

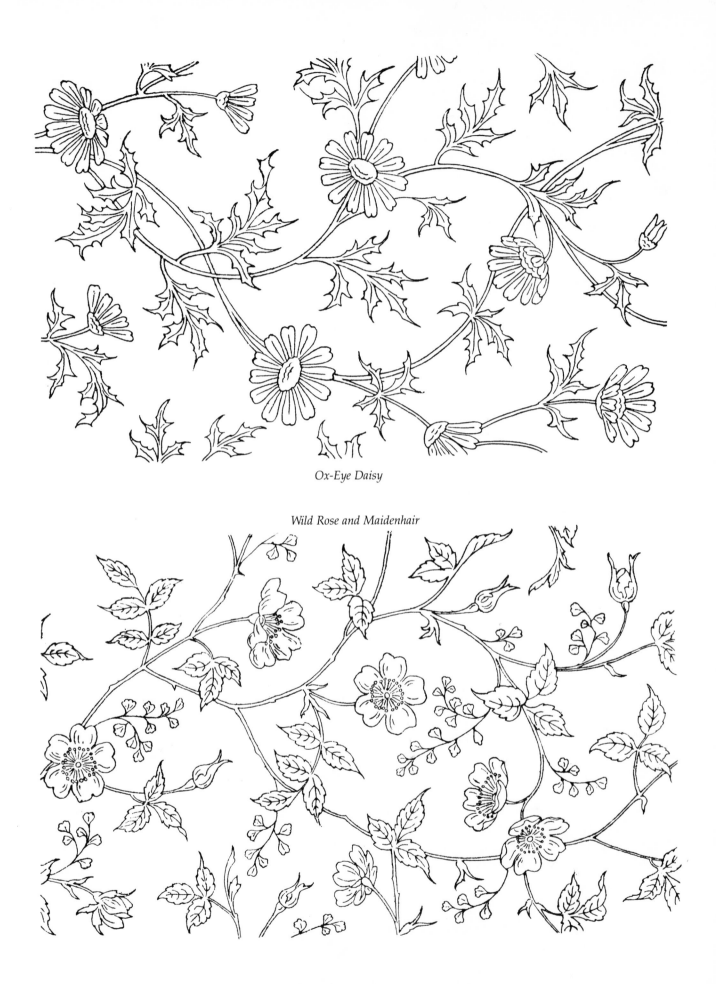

Ox-Eye Daisy

Wild Rose and Maidenhair

Narcissus

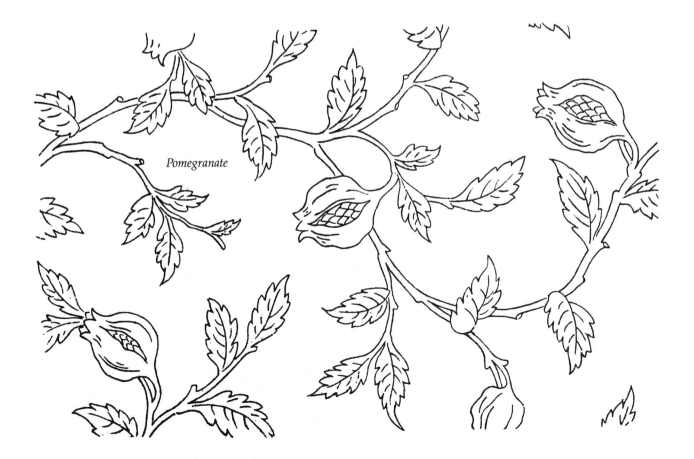

Pomegranate

Single Dahlia

Verbena

Wild Rose

Lily of the Valley

Cornflower

Jessamine

Pansy

Strawberry

Rosebud and Forget-Me-Not

Mountain Ash and Daisy

Primrose

Apple Blossom

Forget-Me-Not and Rosebud

Jessamine and Wild Rose

Jessamine

Jessamine and Fern

Poppy and Corn

Chrysanthemum

Buttercup and Daisy

Lily of the Valley and Fern

Buttercup

Violet

Mixed Ferns

Forget-Me-Not, Rose and Daisy

Virginia Creeper

Forget-Me-Not and Fern

Mountain Ash

Daisy

Poppy and Wheat

Forget-Me-Not

Wild Rose

Rosebud, Jessamine
and Forget-Me-Not

Daisy

Rosebud

Mountain Ash

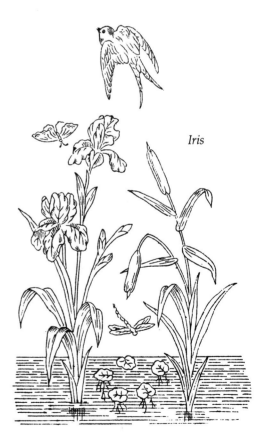

Iris

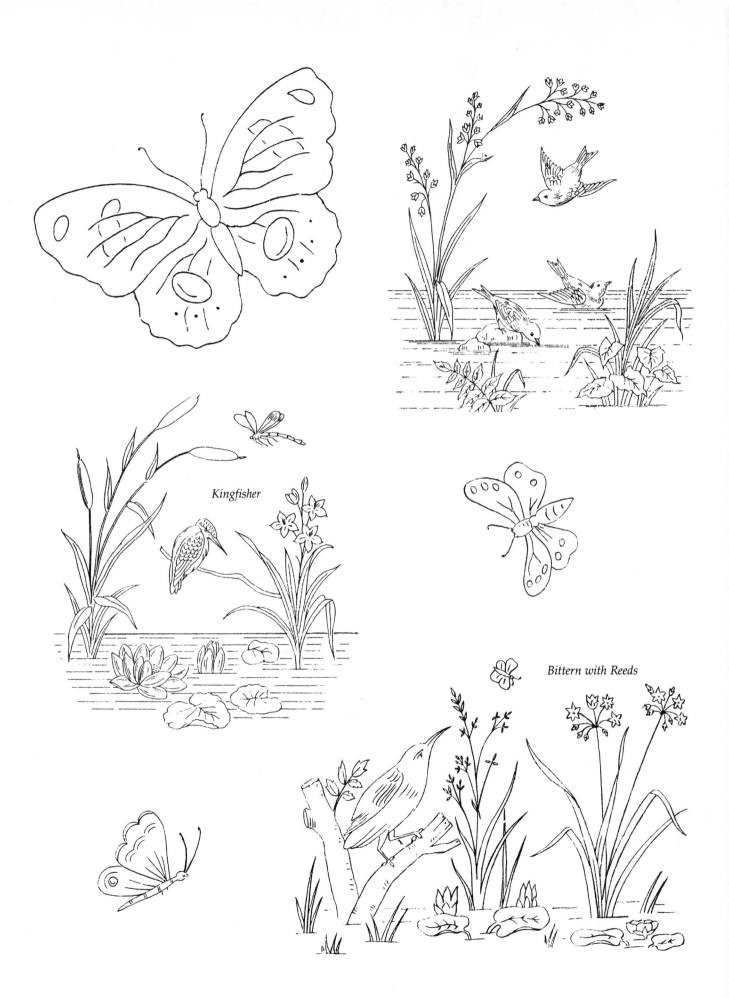

Kingfisher

Bittern with Reeds

Owl

Heron

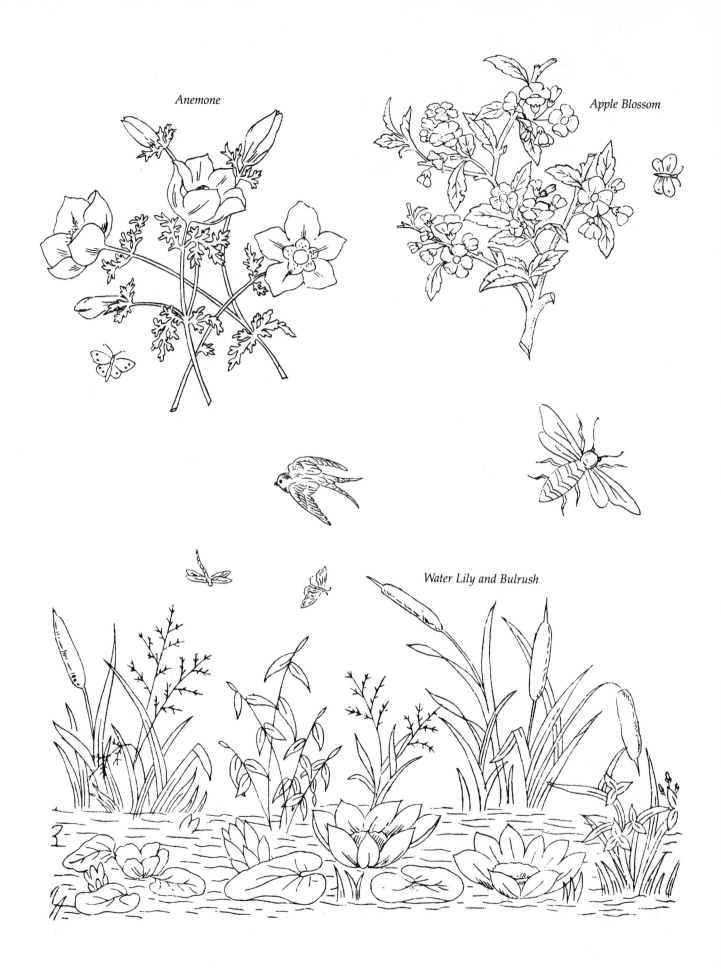

Anemone

Apple Blossom

Water Lily and Bulrush

Swallow

Water Lily and Bulrush

Swallow

Kingfisher

Flamingo with Reeds

Fern

Marguerite Daisy

Water Lily and Bulrush

Water Lily

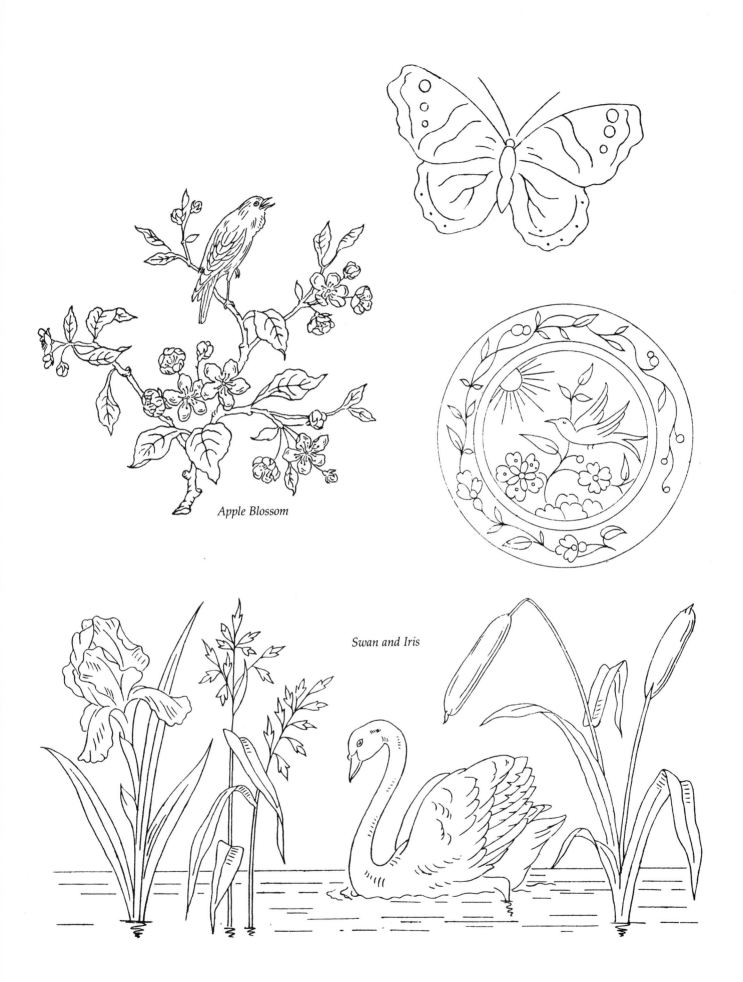

Apple Blossom

Swan and Iris

Holly

Bulrush

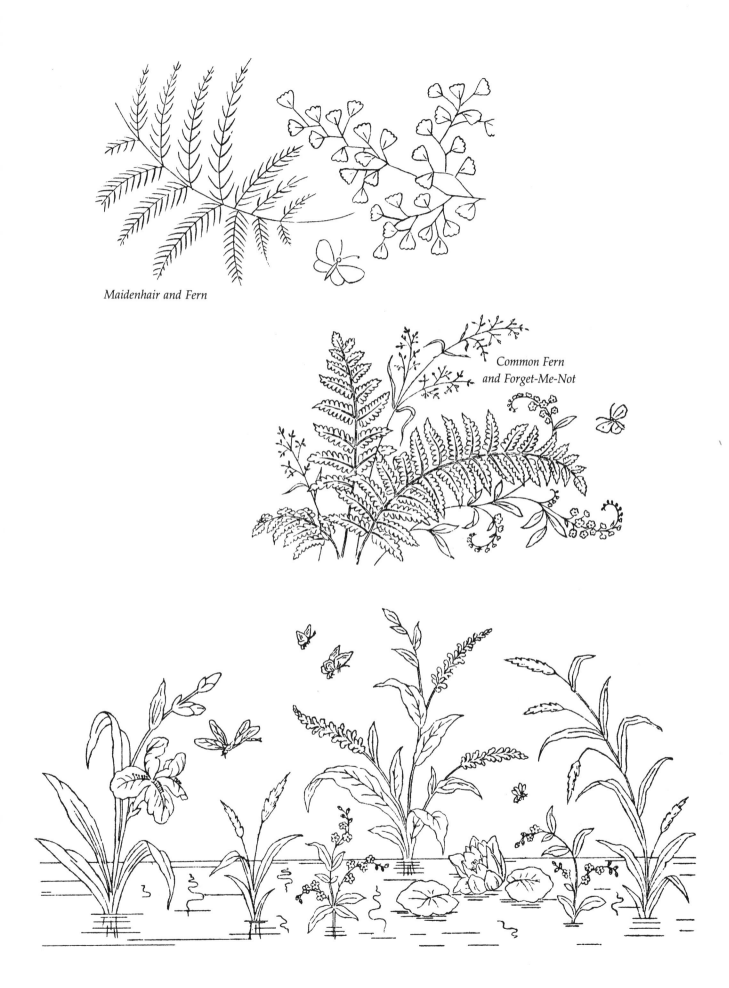

Maidenhair and Fern

*Common Fern
and Forget-Me-Not*

Mixed Ferns

"Scylla" Quilt Square

"Oriental" Quilt Square

"Oriental" Quilt Square

"Fuchsia" Table Center

"Barleycorn" Cushion Square

"Blue-Bud" Quilt Square

"Flowering Rush" Quilt Square

"Crowfoot" Table Cover

"Claudia" Cushion Design

"Crown Derby" Table Center

"Cabrifole" Cushion Square

"Hungarian" Quilt Square

"Priscilla" Cushion Design

"Rococo" Cushion Design

"Ravoise" Cushion Square

Field Daisy Table Center (ribbon-work design)

Apple Blossom Table Center (ribbon-work design)

Conventional Daisy Table Center (ribbon-work design)

Marguerite Table Center (ribbon-work design)

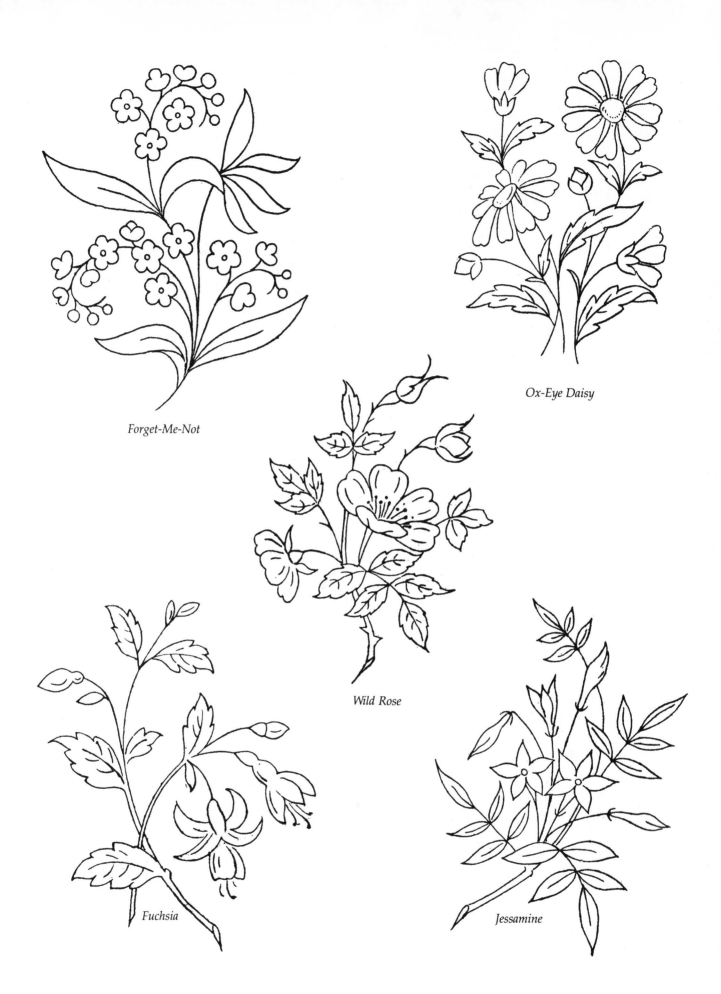

Forget-Me-Not

Ox-Eye Daisy

Wild Rose

Fuchsia

Jessamine

Forget-Me-Not

Crocus and Snowdrop

Narcissus and Geranium

Virginia Creeper

Primrose

"Haarlem" Tulip

Daisy and Fern

Lily

Tiger Lily

Rosebud

Wild Rose and Oats Grass

Holly

Apple Blossom

Ivy

Primrose

Verbena

Pansy

Wild Rose

Lily

Plum

Pansy

Fruit

Daffodil

Poppy, Wheat and Cornflower

Pomegranate

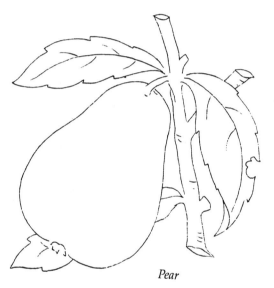

Pear

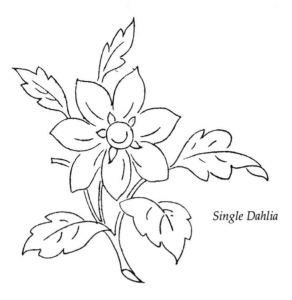

Single Dahlia

Lilium

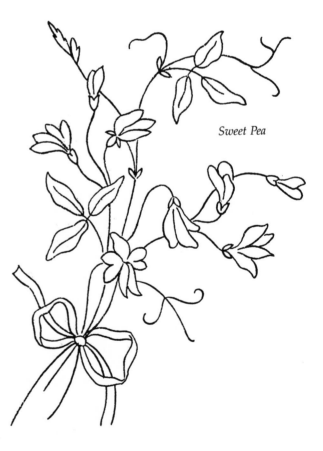

Sweet Pea

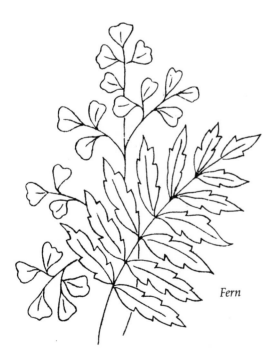

Fern

Single Dahlia

Grape

Blackberry

Strawberry

Lily

Arum Lily

Cornflower

Maidenhair

"Windham" Design

"Damascus" Design

"Rochelle" Design

INDEX OF MOTIFS

Acacia, 6
Acorn, 8
Anemone, 74
Apple blossom, 6, 15, 43, 44, 63, 74, 79, 99, 106
Arum lily, 30, 35
Azalea, 6, 11, 12

"Barleycorn" design, 87
Begonia, 53
Berries, 9
Bittern, 72
Blackberry, 41, 53
"Blue-bud" design, 88
Blush rose, 28
Bulrush, 74, 76, 80
Buttercup, 66

"Caprifole" design, 93
Carnation, 18
Cherry, 9, 15
Chrysanthemum, 65
"Claudia" design, 91
Clover, 48
Cornflower, 7, 62, 116
Crocus, 21, 103
"Crowfoot" design, 90
"Crown Derby" design, 92
Cyclamen, 49

Daffodil, 22, 45, 51, 110
Dahlia, 15, 20, 38, 41, 49, 57, 61
Daisy, 6, 7, 9, 15, 45, 52, 56, 63, 68, 69, 100, 104
    Field, 98
    Marguerite, 9, 19, 23, 77, 101
    Ox-eye, 8, 15, 18, 58, 102
"Damascus" design, 117

Fern, 6, 7, 9, 15, 19, 39, 46, 50, 64, 66, 67, 77, 81
Field daisy, 98

Flamingo, 77
"Flowering Rush" design, 89
Forget-me-not, 7, 8, 9, 14, 21, 35, 51, 63, 64, 67, 69, 81, 82, 102
Fruit, 110
Fuchsia, 9, 18, 19, 86, 102

Geranium, 9, 103

Hawthorn, 6, 53
Hawthorn blossom, 8
Heron, 73
Hibiscus, 21
Holly, 9, 38, 80, 106
"Hungarian" design, 94

Iris, 34, 71, 79
Ivy, 6, 7, 54, 106

Jessamine, 6, 7, 9, 50, 62, 64, 69, 102

Kingfisher, 72, 76

Lilium, 8, 19
    Longiflorum, 12
Lily, 40, 104, 107, 115
    Arum, 30, 35, 115
    Tiger, 104
    Water, 19, 24, 74, 77, 78
Lily of the valley, 61, 65
Lozenge, 16

Maidenhair, 19, 39, 58, 81, 116
Marguerite daisy, 9, 19, 23, 77, 101
Mountain ash, 6, 7, 8, 15, 19, 42, 52, 63, 67, 71

Narcissus, 14, 59, 103

Oats grass, 105
Orange, 14
"Oriental" design, 84, 85

Owl, 73
Ox-eye daisy, 8, 15, 18, 58, 102

Pansy, 6, 25, 56, 62, 107, 110
Passion flower, 8, 36
Pink, 55
Plum, 110
Pomegranate, 21, 59
Poppy, 15, 18, 22, 34, 42, 65, 68, 111
Primrose, 6, 63, 103, 106
"Priscilla" design, 95

"Ravoise" design, 97
Reeds, 72, 77
Renaissance, 14
"Rochelle" design, 117
"Rococo" design, 96
Rose, 9, 23, 24
    Blush, 28
Rosebud, 7, 8, 45, 51, 52, 63, 64, 69, 70, 105

"Scylla" design, 83
Snowdrop, 103
Strawberry, 6, 54, 62
Swallow, 75, 76
Swan, 79
Sycamore, 10

Tiger lily, 104
Tulip, 104

Verbena, 61
Violet, 66
Virginia creeper, 9, 11, 15, 52, 103

Water lily, 19, 24, 74, 76, 77, 78
Wheat, 15, 42, 68, 111
Wild rose, 6, 7, 9, 18, 19, 39, 58, 61, 64, 69, 102, 105, 107
"Windham" design, 116
Winter jasmine, 12